A CORNER OF ENGLAND

A CORNER OF ENGLAND

NORTH DEVON LANDSCAPES AND PEOPLE

James Ravilious

DEVON BOOKS
THE LUTTERWORTH PRESS

First published in 1995 by Devon Books
in association with The Lutterworth Press

CIP Catalogue Record for this book is available from the British Library

*The wood engraving on the half title page is by Eric Ravilious. The lino-cut cockerel is by
Robin Ravilious. Other wood engravings are by Thomas Bewick.
The photograph on the title page shows Ashwell, near Dolton, in autumn.*

DEVON BOOKS
Halsgrove House
Lower Moor Way
Tiverton Devon EX16 6SS
Telephone 01884 243242
Facsimile 01884 243325

ISBN 0 86114 897 5

THE LUTTERWORTH PRESS
PO Box 60, Cambridge CB1 2NT

ISBN 0 71882 943 3

Reprographics by Peninsular Repro Services, Exeter
Printed and bound in England by BPC Wheatons, Exeter

Ashwell, near Dolton, in winter.

Red Devon cows, Narracott, near Hollocombe.

FOREWORD

BY CHRIS CHAPMAN

When I look at James Ravilious's photographs I see much that is familiar. If you asked a writer to describe a bedroom where a bachelor farmer went to bed by candlelight, and they understood what it was to live in the depths of the country, then I'm certain they'd describe James's picture. The alarm clock, the heavy layers of wallpaper that cling to the lime plaster and swallow the damp, the bed with its hollowed mattress and large feather quilt, so warm that you can forget the cold night air as it drifts round the room, and the candle itself, with its gentle light dancing round the ceiling.

James has a rare talent for capturing the commonplace and revealing it as a significant moment in time. Most of us recognise the elements in the photographs. We will have seen the shadow of the church as it stretches across the graveyard, the sheep on a hot day lying fat and contented in the hollow of some old hedge, and that brief tender moment when a farmer acknowledges his love for his dog.

There aren't many photographers who have documented the same area for as many years as he has. Today the camera is thought of as global and the tool of the traveller. It's a credit to him that he has persevered for so long. We now have a visual record of a much loved Devon that is, slowly, passing into history.

But this book is more than just a slice of history, for these are wonderful pictures. Look closely. They've been taken by a warm eye, a subtle sense of humour and, above all, a deep respect for the subject.

Throwleigh, 1995

John Squire, Dolton.

INTRODUCTION

I consider myself lucky to have been able to work, with relative freedom, compiling the Beaford photographic archive in North Devon for seventeen years, from 1973 to 1989. Few photographers can have enjoyed such prolonged patronage in such a nice place! A good deal of that time was spent copying early photographs, so the Beaford Archive consists of two parts, modern pictures complemented by copies of older photographs of the same area.

The Beaford Arts Centre was established by the Dartington Hall Trust in 1966. In 1972, the then Director, John Lane, asked me to continue the recently established record of North Devon life as part of the Centre's continuing programme in the region.

Like many photographers, I much prefer to work in black & white. The fact that colour film will fade and alter with time means that it is not really suitable for archival use. However, it seemed a shame to ignore colour altogether, especially the gay decorations in local villages on Royal occasions and fetes, or the true colour of the local breed of cattle, the Devon Red. I therefore took some colour for my own satisfaction. This sort of photography is a mixture of planning and luck, sometimes you plan (with or without success); sometimes a subject falls into your lap. All but six of the black & white photographs chosen for this book are selected from the Archive, and I hope they form a representative selection, rather like scenes from a tapestry I have been stitching over the years.

What inspires me most is 'ordinary life' – which of course is never ordinary. I never set up photographs, preferring to take life as it comes. For pleasure and support I look at paintings more than photographs, though I particularly admire the work of Henri Cartier-Bresson, and the marvellous books of Olive Cook and Edwin Smith. Another inspiration is the work of the wood-engraver Thomas Bewick, undoubtedly the best record of English country life ever made. Although he worked in Northumberland in the eighteenth century, I am sure he would have found much to inspire him in this part of Devon.

On the technical side, I have always used Leica range-finder cameras, and prefer the character and quality of their earlier uncoated lenses. Most of my photographs were taken with a 35mm, wide angle lens, together with a Yellow '0' filter for clouds. I have used standard 400 ISO film and strongly recommend compensation development. This means rating the film at, say, 200 ISO and under-developing to compensate for this over-exposure. This gives a far superior tonal quality to negatives, which are consequently much easier to print. I wish I had discovered this earlier in my career! For colour I use Kodachrome 25, with an 81A filter. I think I should also add a word of warning to photographers here – after many years in the darkroom I have become sensitized to the chemicals and react to them, even after only a few minutes exposure, so please take heed of the manufacturer's warnings and make sure your darkroom has adequate ventilation.

A positive result of this misfortune is that since giving up darkroom work I have spent two years putting all the information about my photographs on to a computer database; I cannot say how wonderful it is for me, (and hopefully the general public too), to be able to find things quickly at the touch of a few buttons! I would like to thank Janis and Fred of Keystroke Computing, Crediton, and Athos Pittordou for their invaluable help and advice in setting this up. I will shortly start to computerise the information on the early photographs.

Both parts of the Archive are now housed at the North Devon Record Office in Barnstaple. I would like to pay tribute to the late Louise Rose, Senior Archivist, whose unfailingly cheerful support made the initial move there so easy and pleasant, and to thank her partner Hans for his help in building the darkroom.

Since Louise's tragic death, her successor, Tim Wormleighton, and his staff, have continued to be most supportive. The Beaford Archive is now in the capable hands of the photographer Bryony Harris, who has always been such a pleasure to work with. I would like to thank her for printing the photographs for this book, with such care and patience, in a very sticky heat wave!

Warmest thanks to Chris Chapman, and Tony Foster, and to Common Ground, whose inspiration and friendship has meant such a lot to me, particularly in difficult times; also to Beryl Cheesman, Gareth Keene, Rosemary Lyons of North Devon District Council, Simon Timms of Devon County Council, Ron Hill of The North Devon Journal, and Chas Halsey at Focal Point, for all their help. Sponsorship from Elmgrant, and Chartered Accountants, Glover Pearce & Ross, is also greatly appreciated. Finally, I would like to say how much Robin and I have enjoyed working with all the staff at Devon Books and, in particular, Karen Binaccioni who designed this book.

This book is dedicated to my wife Robin, and Ben and Ella, my children, who have put up with so much over the years, and to the marvellous people of North Devon, who made the job such a constant pleasure.

James Ravilious
Autumn, 1995

The Beaford Archive, as part of the Beaford Centre, is supported by South West Arts, Devon County Council, North Devon District Council, Torridge District Council, Torrington Town Council, Dartington North Devon Foundation and Torrington Town Lands, Alms and Poors Charities.

Early morning from Ashreigney church tower.

Cob barn, Ingleigh Green.

PREFACE

The corner of England celebrated in these pictures is a small patch of North Devon, roughly 20 miles across, which spans the valleys of two rivers, the Torridge and the Taw. This is the area in which James did most of his recording for the Beaford Archive – the immediate countryside round the Beaford Centre and our home in nearby Dolton.

I was bred and born in this region, and have loved it all my life. Luckily, James fell in love with it too, and so, soon after we married, we moved from London to the tiny cob-and-thatch cottage my grandfather had given me.

It was the people and places I had known since birth, therefore, that became James's first subjects. But his field expanded rapidly through everyday connections, and the local grapevine, or simply by pottering through the lanes – a favourite pastime for us both.

His task was an extraordinary one: to record the look of the place and its people, their work, play, and special occasions, and above all, the whole texture of their everyday lives. Anything was relevant. He was, as it were, perpetually 'on call'. It was hardly a regular job, but full of interest and surprise. Sometimes he was out at dawn to catch a scene in the early light. Sometimes he was hours late for lunch, having spotted a photogenic subject over a gate. Sometimes he came home frozen, having stood all morning on a windy hilltop, waiting for a travelling cloud shadow to reach the perfect spot. For me, there was constant delight as each new piece of my beloved countryside was captured forever.

The special quality of this part of Devon is hard to define. A great many trees – in woods, dishevelled hedges, and odd corners of scrub – create a sense of wildness and neglect. The misty Western light is often sad. In the secret combes and wooded river valleys one can feel remote from the modern world. Perhaps the pervading sense is of gentle melancholy.

It is a man-made landscape, but an ancient one. Its field patterns composed less by eighteenth century enclosure, than by the first settlers of the twelfth century, hacking their quirky bits and pieces out of the moorland and forest. Avoiding difficult obstacles rather than removing them, these pioneers made lanes and boundaries that wriggle across the hills with as much abandon as the multitude of streams.

The early settlers also gave us the great hedge-banks which are still such a feature here: broad earth banks topped with hawthorn to keep out wild deer. Many of these ancient boundaries remain. Now colonized by other trees and shrubs, they make a tracery of living copse across the cultivated land. Formerly, they were controlled and strengthened by 'laying' the living branches horizontally. Now they are more often cut by machine till they grow threadbare; or simply left to flourish as they please. Many a North Devon lane in early summer is a tunnel of leaves and flowers in which one can get deliciously lost, for the signposts are often baffling, and the distant view comes only in a tantalizing glimpse, through a gateway, of blue hills and faraway church towers.

There are, in any case, few major destinations here. Most industry and tourism bypasses this country, heading for Barnstaple, Bideford, or the coastal resorts. Within it, the chief communities are three smallish market towns: Hatherleigh, Torrington, and Chulmleigh. The myriad lanes link hilltop villages and their out-lying farms.

In such a landscape, change moves slowly; agri-business is little suited here. The small mixed farm is the commonest unit still. Short of labour, short of capital, bothered by paperwork and recession, farmers struggle on stoically in a cold soil, high rain-fall, and awkward upland terrain, much as their predecessors have done for generations.

The positive side of this, however, is that much of the old rural way of life survives – a bit decayed perhaps – but still clearly visible for the camera to record. Cob houses and barns with their humble, irregular lines not yet smartened up. Pavements and yards still cobbled with river pebbles. Old customs, crafts, and festivals kept going. Wheat is grown for thatching straw,

dried in the age-old stooks, and built into old-fashioned ricks till the reed-comber comes. And people treasure old ways. For it is in the local character to hold on to the past, in the midst of accelerating change, recalling its hardships and its pleasures with mingled wonder and regret.

It was the traditional subjects, picturesque and vulnerable as they are, which attracted James's eye especially – in some cases, only just in time. A few have vanished altogether since he recorded them. The great elms of farmyard and hedgerow are dead. The battered metal milk churns have gone from the farm gate. And some of the finest old cob threshing barns have sunk back into the earth from which they came. (It is a curious thought that whatever he has recorded – however humdrum, or 'new-fangled' now – may one day be pored over with pangs of nostalgia, or amused disbelief!).

As James's pictures show, this is a special landscape with an elegiac beauty all its own. It is also a rich subject for an archive, being one of the last regions where the English rural tradition is still alive. Few of the others – if any – have been recorded in such depth.

Robin Ravilious
Autumn, 1995

Reg Holland, New House, near Chulmleigh.

Early morning mist on the River Torridge near Dolton.

Early morning mist on the River Taw near Chulmleigh.

Near the source of the River Taw, looking North.

Homeland Bridge on the River Taw near Eggesford.

Beech stump at Spittle, near Chulmleigh.

Looking South-West across the region from Five Barrows, Exmoor.

Eileen Squire setting up stooks near Dolton.

Stooks and rainbow, Westacott, Riddlecombe.

Alf Pugsley, Lower Langham, near Dolton.

Arthur Ford, Wood Farm, near Dolton.

Ivor Brock, Millhams, Dolton.

George Stoneman, Skellies, Riddlecombe.

Old oak tree in blizzard, near Dolton.

Muddy field at Ingleigh Green.

Flock of geese, Indiwell, near Swimbridge.

The River Torridge near Beaford.

Woodricks at Cupper's Piece, near Beaford.

Irwin Piper leading his flock, Upcott, near Dolton.

Stephen Middleton watering sheep, Westacott, Riddlecombe.

Archie Parkhouse's shed collapsed in the great blizzard, Millhams, Dolton, 1978.

Poultry in snow, Cupper's Piece, near Beaford.

Poultry farm at Middlemoor, near Bondleigh.

Jo Curzon milking her goat, Millhams, Dolton.

Red Devon cow, Narracott, near Hollocombe.

Morley King on his tractor, Middle Week, near Iddesleigh.

Netting cabbages, Lower Langham, near Dolton.

Simon Berry loading a linkbox, Harepath, near Beaford.

Bullocks in a meadow, Lower Langham, near Dolton.

Apple tree at Millhams, Dolton.

Approaching storm, Ramscliffe, near Beaford.

Bringing in a sick lamb, Densham, near Ashreigney.

Pigs by a woodrick, Parsonage Farm, Iddesleigh.

Goats in a meadow, Millhams, Dolton.

Cow in a shippen window, Parsonage Farm, Iddesleigh.

Store cattle, Parsonage Farm, Chulmleigh.

View across the Torridge valley to Merton.

Bramble.

Orchard at West Park, Iddesleigh

Snowdrops at Cupper's Piece, near Beaford.

Lost sheep in a lane, Millhams, Dolton.

George Ayre and Jo Curzon spraying a shorn lamb, Addisford, Dolton.

John Moyes bottle-feeding lambs, Brookland, near Chulmleigh.

Sheep resting in the heat of May, Halsdon, near Dolton.

Archie Parkhouse and his pig, Millhams, Dolton.

Bill Cooke and his cows, Colehouse, near Riddlecombe.

Archie Parkhouse in his lambing shed, Millhams, Dolton.

Archie Parkhouse and his dog, Sally, Millhams, Dolton.

Alf Pugsley moving a shed in case of flood,
Lower Langham, near Dolton.

Archie Parkhouse and Ivor Brock dragging home a sick ram, Millhams, Dolton.

Phil Gent cleaning out a ditch, Mousehole, near Iddesleigh.

Picking up potatoes, Westacott, Riddlecombe.

Ralph Hunkin cutting sileage, Long Cross, Black Torrington.

Rams in the orchard, West Park, Iddesleigh.

Farm implements in an orchard, Satterleigh.

Muck-spreading, Ashreigney.

Jo Curzon with orphan lambs, Millhams, Dolton.

Bridge Town, near Iddesleigh.

Bluebells, Rushleigh Copse, near Dolton.

Ruined water-mill, West Park, Iddesleigh.

Cow and cob barn, Middle Week, near Iddesleigh.

Mooing cow in a gateway, Ashwell, near Dolton.

Thatched house at Upcott, near Dolton.

Ruined cob barn, Hawkridge, near Coldridge.

Tractor in nettles.

Farmhouse window ledge.

Farm porch, Northlew.

Young bulls eating thistle heads.

Jo Curzon's turkeys.

Reedcombing at Spittle, near Chulmleigh.

The shadow of Ashreigney church – early morning.

Bill Hammond thatching a rick, Westacott, Riddlecombe.

Reedcombing at Westacott, Riddlecombe.

Combine-harvester at Huish Barton, near Merton.

Carrying bales at twilight, Iddesleigh.

Farmer going home, Bray valley, near South Molton.

John Ward ploughing, Parsonage Farm, Iddesleigh.

Seymour Husbands ploughing with horses, Sandy Park, Charles.

A farmer's breakfast table.

Farm interior near Black Torrington.

The French family watching the Cup Final, Brendon Barton, Exmoor.

Wilfie Spiers pouring tea, Mount Pleasant, Beaworthy.

Archie Parkhouse and his cow, Millhams, Dolton.

Herbert Snell mending a sluice-gate at Head Mill, King's Nympton.

Sue Mills, Unigate Milk Factory, Torrington – on the last day churns were in use.

Wilf Butt thatching, Winkleigh.

Dick Smith shearing, Chulmleigh.

The Stevenstone Hunt arriving at a meet, Halsdon, Dolton.

Listening for the hounds, near Halsdon, Dolton.

A kill by the Torrington Farmers' Hunt near Hatherleigh.

View of West Park farm and Iddesleigh village.

Millhams cottages near Dolton.

View towards Dartmoor from Hatherleigh churchyard.

Early morning, Roborough.

Post vans at Winkleigh.

Buddle Lane, Hatherleigh.

Tom Heddon fetching his newspaper, Hatherleigh.

Main street, Black Torrington.

Village oak and garage, Burrington.

Dorothy Hiscock on her milk round, West Lane, Dolton.

Rowena Hoare, teacher, and children of Chulmleigh
Primary School, going to the sports field.

South Molton Street, Chulmleigh – early morning.

Fore Street, Chulmleigh.

Milk churns by a house in Sheepwash.

Mill Street, Torrington.

Children waiting for the school bus near Huish.

After school, Hatherleigh.

Jean Harris, teacher, and Leigh Hiscock,
Chulmleigh Primary School.

Mrs Agate, a grandmother, is introduced to
the new computer, Dolton Primary School.

Ike Jewell collecting his pension, Appledore.

Cheese stall, Barnstaple Pannier Market.

Les Smale's motor-bike showroom, Torrington.

Bill Cooke in his kitchen, Colehouse, near Riddlecombe.

Ivy Badcock in her kitchen, Beaford.

Gracie Fursdon and her dresser, Hatherleigh.

Eve Lynch-Blosse, North Ham, Dolton.

Michael Davis, retired solicitor, Dolton.

Archie Parkhouse shaving, Dolton.

Miss Steele and Mrs Laperriere, Dolton.

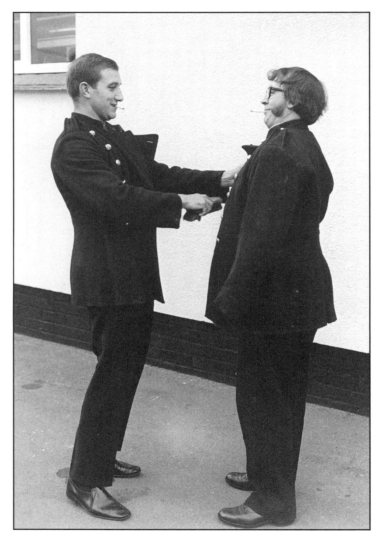

Hatherleigh firemen, Geoff Brooks and Tony Cook.

Tramp camping near Dolton.

Going home from cricket practice, Chulmleigh.

Elizabeth Wescott and her spacehopper,
Higher House, near Atherington.

Cottage interior, Monkokehampton.

Cottage interior, Mariansleigh.

Wilfie Spiers' bedroom, Mount Pleasant, Beaworthy.

Beatrice Clapworthy selling daffodils, Small Marsh, High Bickington.

Nurse Mary Woods weighing a new baby, Addisford, Dolton.

Dr Paul Bangay visiting a patient at Langtree.

Dr. Richard Westcott talking to a patient, Thomas Wright, at Chittlehamholt.

Dr. Richard Westcott listening to Bill Brown's chest, South Molton.

Bruce Evydean adding to an inscription, Beaford churchyard.

Eugene Badcock, printer, Barnstaple.

Bert Heard, builder, in his workshop, Dolton.

Reg Badcock, nursery gardener, School Lane, Torrington.

Salmon fishermen mending nets, Bideford.

Doris May, last of the wooden fishing boats, Bideford.

Trapnell's drapers' shop, High Street, Bideford.

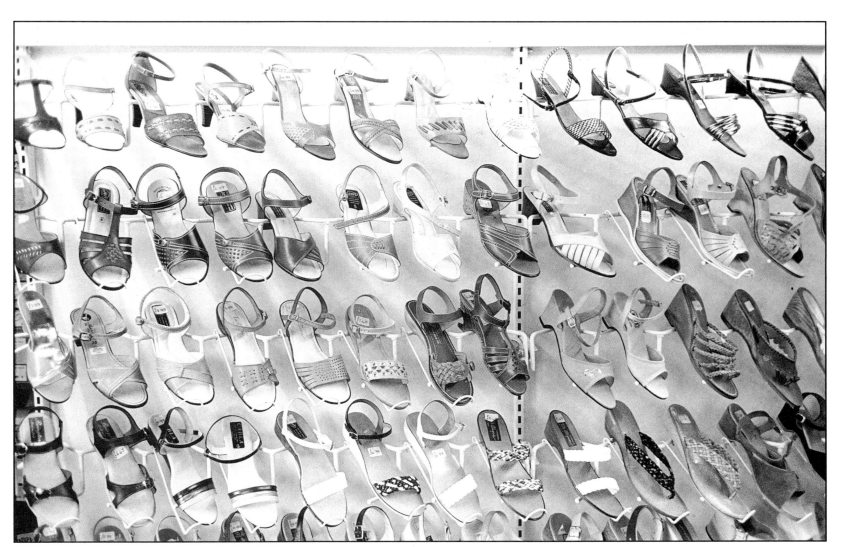

Shoe display, Taylor's shoe shop, Mill Street, Bideford.

Sale at Chapple , Langham.

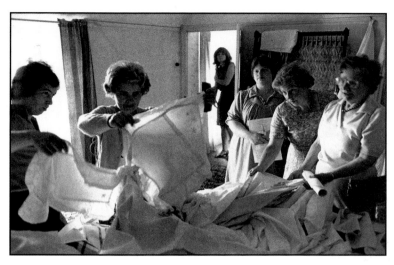

Viewing household linen at a sale, Dolton.

Cottage sale, near Roborough.

Paul and Diane Foggo, auctioneers, selling china, Dolton.

129

Jean Clements and her champion cat, Torrington.

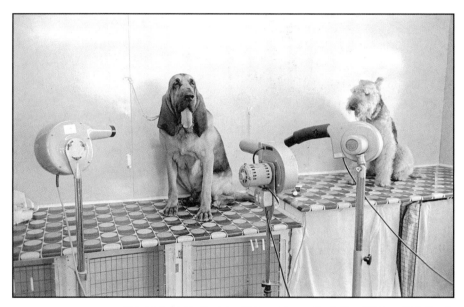

Drying dogs, Bonny Pets parlour, East-the-Water, Bideford.

The kitchen garden, Merton Rectory.

Village scene, Northlew.

Edward Cowle in his garden, Winkleigh.

Bill Folland and Bill Cooke "skinning rods"– stripping willow
for basket-making, Riddlecombe.

Bill Hutchins hoeing potatoes, Dolton.

Queenie Knight in her garden, near Black Torrington.

Michael Mitchell's entries for Dolton Flower Show.

The Friend family cleaning up the churchyard, Dolton.

The churchyard at Shobrooke.

Churchyard steps at Winkleigh.

Picking ivy for Easter decorations, Merton churchyard.

Wedding of Alida Pickard and Nigel Pollard, Dolton.

The Revd. Peter Douglas christening Tina Chastey, Inwardleigh.

Bridesmaid, Chulmleigh.

Bride and groom after their wedding, Dolton.

Evelyn Folland decorating Dowland church.

The Revd. "Bill" Smyth collecting money
at the Roborough Revel.

Dot Heard playing the organ in Dolton Baptist Chapel.

Waiting for the Harvest Supper.

Chulmleigh Congregational Church's Harvest Festival:
singing hymns after the Harvest Supper.

Recording the Royal Wedding celebrations
(on a box camera), Iddesleigh, 1981.

Remembrance Sunday parade, Chulmleigh.

Women's Institute Christmas play, High Bickington.

Women's Institute play, Merton.

Florence Heaman washing up, Over-60's Club, Dolton.

Tea ladies at a Women's Institute talk,
John Gay Room, Barnstaple.

Baby Show at Chulmleigh Church Fete.

Sister Irene Morris judging the Baby Competition, Chulmleigh Fair.

Soft fruit section, Dolton Flower Show.

Cecil Denford with the Hatherleigh Church
Sunday School garland.

154

Hatherleigh Band parading at the Carnival.

The Mayor's parade, Torrington May Fair.

Joanne Durk, Royal Wedding Day, Dolton, 1981.

Mary Middleton, Dolton Carnival Queen
(and husband Paul as a devil).

Elsie Brayley crowning Sandra Ford as Chulmleigh Fair Queen.

Waiting for the Carnival parade, Hartland

Fete at Torridge View Residential Home, Torrington.

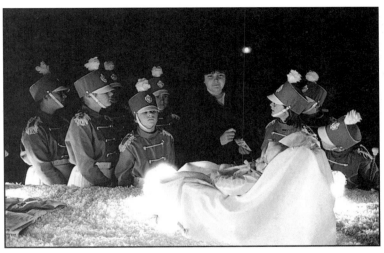

Majorettes at Dolton Carnival.

Cavaliers and Wombles entertaining at a Gymkhana
for Riding for the Disabled, Torrington.

Prize-winning float, "Dougal", Torrington May Fair.

Presenting commemorative mugs, Ashreigney, Royal Wedding Day, 1981.